LIVING BEHIND THE SHADOW

The Life Story of the Niece of Daisy Gatson-Bates

By Mia Gatson

KINGDOM NEWS TODAY
Publication Services, LLC

Living Behind the Shadow
The Life Story of the Niece of Daisy Gatson-Bates

Copyright © 2019, Mia Gatson.
Contact the Author via e-mail at <u>cleandreagatson@icloud.com</u>

All rights reserved. No part of this book may be reproduced, stored in a retrieved system, or transmitted in any form or any means, electronic, mechanical, photocopying, recording, scanning, or otherwise, without the prior written permission of the author.

Author: Mia Gatson

Editor & Publication Services:
Kingdom News Publication Services, LLC.

DISCLAIMER
All the material contained in this book is provided for educational and informational purposes only. No responsibility can be taken for any results or outcomes resulting from the use of this material.

While every attempt has been made to provide information that is both accurate and effective, the author does not assume any responsibility for the accuracy or use/misuse of this information.

Printed in the United States of America.
ISBN 978-0998026268

DEDICATION

This book is dedicated to my sons, Samuel and Emanuel. They kept me breathing when I wanted to stop. It was their honesty, love and admiration for me, their mother that kept me going. They both pushed me be and do greater. My greatest accomplishment will always be raising two young men who are forever evolving into a greatness that can never be measured. Despite their personal challenges with Samuel being on the autism spectrum and Emanuel who wasn't supposed to live, they both are fighters. God had a plan and it will not return void. I am excited to see them live out God's will for their lives.

I would also like to acknowledge, Ernest, my best friend and confidant. I thank you for loving me past my pain.

Mia & Aunt Daisy

Mia's 16th Birthday Celebration

TABLE OF CONTENTS

Chapter 1: What's Missing? 1

Chapter 2: What's Not Working? 8

Chapter 3: Momma, How Do I Look? 15

Chapter 4: Recognizing the Legacy 21

Chapter 5: How Did I Get Off Track? 25

Chapter 6: Where is the Help? 31

Chapter 7: Moving Past the Hurt and Brokenness 35

Chapter 8: It's Not Over Yet 41

Chapter 9: Aunt Daisy's Lessons 45

Chapter 10: She Led Me to Him 53

Chapter 11: Block Out Noises of Negativity 59

Chapter 12: Moving Beyond the Shadow 66

Poem of Encouragement 70

CHAPTER 1

What's Missing?

I often wonder where my life would be if my aunt hadn't been called home so early. Would I have this awesome life, never having to worry about money or struggling from day to day? Where would I live? Who would I be married to? Certainly, I know I wouldn't have gone through three marriages.

When people hear me ponder these questions out loud, they look at me as though I have some sort of disease and that it was my plan to have a weird life. I'm not sure how people look at me now, but I do know that I don't care! Sometimes, I begin to ask myself, is this an issue, or is it mental illness or is it just the stress of being free.

Yes, there is stress with being free. What is it? This happens when people not understand you or your story, constantly wondering who you really are and what your problem is. You end up going out alone, eating alone, to movies and events alone. This can be and is stressful because you don't have anyone you fully trust to talk to or do social things with. Sometimes it even feels like you're just existing and going through the motions of life, with no real interaction with people. Also, because people don't understand you, you make a choice to stay to yourself so you don't have to continually explain yourself, which is exhausting as well.

My aunt wouldn't be satisfied with what or who I've become. It's not good enough I know that, but it's all I have right now and that's what we have to focus on, the right now. Sometimes the in between is better to look at than the end. Last night, I went to my son's game and I had to I borrow $4.00 to get in and couldn't even buy a soda or a piece of candy. I was thankful for the opportunity to see my son play and the fact I couldn't get a refreshment didn't really matter. One thing about me is I see what's ahead, so I don't get stressed out about the right now. I know better days are already here, I just have to stay focused on the details and press forward.

Yes, the details! We can get so caught up on the bigger picture that the small details no longer matter to us. Happiness, your happiness is in the details. As I move through my life, I am constantly asking myself questions. Questions like, Is this my destiny? Or is this a distraction? If we can learn to take the time to answer these questions sincerely, we wouldn't waste so much time. So many times, we want to hold on to things in our life that we know aren't right for us. That is why we answer these questions the way we want to so we can justify those things we know aren't right. But sincere, truthful answers will get us to where we need to be quick.

Here is a question many may ask themselves, "How did I come out?" But the real question that will help you is, "How did I get in?" Get in the abuse, in the bad marriage, in this debt? Most

Living Behind the Shadow

would say low self-esteem. Not for me. I knew who I was. I knew I was beautiful. People had told me all my life. But I didn't know my worth. I didn't know my abilities; I didn't see the structure that basically had been handed to me. So, I lived a mediocre life and always got mediocre results. In every aspect of my life. People tell you to know your worth but that's it. They never give the DETAILS! That's where your happiness lies, in the details. How did I get in? Not knowing my worth, what is my worth? My worth is waking up every morning with a renewed mind. It's having the strength to get up and move forward in WHATEVER SITUATION I'm in. My worth is NOT SETTLING. My worth is smiling through my pain because God has chosen me to breath in the air of THIS day that I will never breathe in again. No matter what your situation is know your worth, know that you're more than who they think you are.

How did I come out? I remembered my worth.

So, you were a First Lady? Yea, how did that work out? It didn't! My husband of four years was emotionally abusive, physically unaware and

Living Behind the Shadow

a constant reminder of what settling actually meant. I wasn't happy, I don't believe I ever was. I just thought it was time to settle down from the life I was living. Drug use, partying, out and up all night, never resting and always on the go. I had no idea that this would be called my manic state of the mental illness that went untreated most of my life. I wouldn't say unnoticed because anyone could see. Well, anyone who really cared, they could see that I was in need of some major help.

It took my ten-year-old getting sick and a week-long hospital stay with a caring nurse to see that something wasn't right. But to that later, for now (staying focused), lets discuss the "Pastor."

I had no idea that he had no running water, no gas and his home was falling apart when I said "I do." I quickly learned that I was just a way for him to get back on his feet. He started out nice as I'm sure all abusers do, but in the end, I didn't even recognize who I was, mentally or physically. Things changed early in our marriage, then I began to wonder was it possible for someone to be so cold and mean. For almost four years I had been mentally broken down. I went from 130 to well over 200 pounds over the course of this paper union. I listened to him talk so negative about the members who would have given their left arm for him. There were some Sundays when the church had no heat and we had to sit in the cold with our coats on listening to him preach about the faith. He was preaching about it, but wasn't living a life of faith. The people would give and sow, but he took and was not honorable with what was given.

When it came to the end of our marriage, I was almost 300 pounds. All the abuse that had taken place within this relationship took a toll on my physical body as well as my mental and spiritual being. He never tried to put on a front, everyone knew his attitude but dared not cross him. I never understood why. To me he was always a man trying or attempting to be something he wasn't. He gave a big talk with nothing to back it up.

Since home was no longer bearable, I began to focus on ministry. The church. I started a number of ministries that really got the people excited and we all were willing to work. However, it was

Living Behind the Shadow

never enough and eventually envy started coming. When envy comes, we often see it coming from the pews, but what I was experiencing was coming from the pulpit.

He hated me. He hated that the people loved me. He hated that God was speaking to me and not to him. He hated my ability to draw the people with the words God had giving me and not him. He hated me and everything I stood for. The people knew. They could see the hate; they could smell the envy and eventually I would be confronted by my enemy to sit down or play his game. I chose neither and this is why I am telling my story today.

CHAPTER 2

What's Not Working?

One day he said to me, "This isn't working." I responded by saying, "What's not working?" The answer I received from his crushed my heart and my spirit literally fell, shattered and broke into a million little pieces. He said, "This marriage." He said it in a way that now makes me wonder if he ever knew God. I heard the words and I stood there as if I was a ghost in spirit. I could no longer feel my flesh, I was still.

As he walked out the door I began to cry out and ask God to give me strength. I didn't ask why. I

Living Behind the Shadow

already knew. He hated my strength. The strength I didn't know I had. He was simply jealous of my anointing.

Hurt, broken and confused on my next move, I stood trying to gather my thoughts feelings. But was unable to because the person I was looking at walked away quickly. I took a couple of steps laid down on the bed and seems like the air I was breathing was no longer available. I laid there and I heard the front door closed. He had left.

At one time the ministry was growing, but because the leader was greedy it didn't last. We had programs like any other church, but I can't tell you where the money went. We were in a cult and didn't even know it.

While these thoughts were rolling through my head, I heard the door opened again. He was coming back. He was a heavy-set man so I could hear his heavy footsteps walking in the house. This moment they seemed heavier. It was almost like I could hear the anger and hate walking through each leg. He appeared at my feet like a wounded baby rabbit. Then he asked, "So when do you think you will be leaving?" I was in shock and didn't even know where all this was coming from.

When you go through the most life changing experiences in your life, there is a place your mind goes and your spirit takes over. That's what happened to me at that moment. I heard myself say give me three days. I didn't know where I was going, I called my mom and she didn't ask any questions. It was like she already knew. She heard the hurt in my voice and knew not to ask questions. Questions at this time would probably force me to go into places I wasn't yet ready to face. I can't tell you much about the rest of that day because it's all a blur.

The next thing I needed to do was to speak to my boys. They were age ten and twelve, but to my surprise they were excited. They never liked him. He never took the time to really get to know them but why should he, they were his step children? He didn't even know his own children and to this day the relationship with his three girls is strained.

It's crazy when I think back, I think of the power we could have had, what we could have built, what we could have had. Now, I laugh because the enemy thought he did something, but what he didn't realize was that I was the blessing and now I speak for myself.

On the third day after receiving notice from my husband that our marriage is not working, I had everything that belonged to me and my two boys packed and ready for the UHAUL. He was kind enough to give me the three days I requested. My boys and I had cried so that our eyes were puffy and I know mine were almost swollen shut. I had packed everything up myself and I was tired, my bones ached and my hope in Christ had faded. I had two beds I needed to get so I could attempt to start to put my life back together. I didn't know how to take them apart, frustrated, tired and somewhat devastated I began to cry yet again. I began to wonder how the great niece of a nationally known icon Daisy Gatson-Bates get in a predicament like this. My mind started to wonder, I thought about the sacrifices I had made, how I worshiped, how I loved, and to have God do me like this was a slap in the face. I begin to pray. I told God if you don't send me an angel right now IM DONE. I'm done with church, I'm done with worship, and I'm done with you. I meant every last word. I cried so hard. It was like I wasn't me. It was an out of body experience, but something in me said you still have to get those beds. So, I stood up feeling like someone else had taken over my body, but I walked outside. I couldn't tell you why, but that's what I did.

When I walked outside, I saw a man walking up the street. I felt like; ok, you need those beds taken down so ask him! I hollered across the street, "Sir, can you help me? Today is my last day to get this stuff out and I have two beds that I don't know how to take down." This man gave me the oddest look, l can't explain it. I figured he wanted money so I went in my pocket and pulled out my last twenty-dollar bill. I said, "Sir, I have twenty dollars I just need your help," and the man shot across the street like he was on fire and said, "Ma'am what do you need?" I showed him the beds and said, "I just need to take them down and get them on the UHAUL and I'll be done." This man worked fast, rearranged my UHAUL, took

Living Behind the Shadow

the beds down, put them on the truck and before I knew it, I was ready to go.

I pulled the twenty dollars out of my pocket and went to hand it to him, I said, "Sir, I thank you for helping me." He looked at me and said, "Ma'am I can't take that." I said, "Why, you have been such a help to me, you didn't have to and I want you to know I thank you."

He said, "I can't take it."

In inquired again why he couldn't take it. Then he said, "If I told you, you wouldn't believe me." I told him, "Sir I have been married to a pastor for the past four years, gave all I had to the marriage, his church, children and family. Most of them did not like me. If you tell me it's raining meat, I'm going in the house to get bread. Please tell me."

He started to tell me his story by saying, "Well about three weeks ago I got laid off from my job, and every day about this time I go to the river to talk to the Lord, but this time when I went, I heard the spirit say get up, go down the street and you're going to see a UHAUL, I need you to help her."

MY GOD! I looked at this man with tears in my eyes. I said, "Sir you are my angel. I just prayed for you." God did that to restore my faith. He knew that I was on my last leg and that I had been broken, but He was letting me know that He had my back and I had not been forgotten. That's what He will do. He will keep you when you want to give up and go back. Remember your worth.

CHAPTER 3

Momma, How Do I Look?

As momma fluffed the ruffles on my favorite red shirt and made sure my curls were in place, I wondered what all the fuss was about. What the big deal was? Why were we on the carport of this stranger's house and what was it about her that my mother felt the need to make a big fuss?

While momma gave me one more look over, I held my doll even tighter. As the door opened, I could see what seemed to be a tall, small frame, light skinned woman with curls just as tight as mine, red lipstick and a blue and white polka dot dress, open the door. She had the most beautiful smile on her face and she quickly said, "Come on in."

Walking into her home felt like I was walking into a magazine. I had a feeling I had never had before. It was nothing short of amazing. Spotless, furniture that would be considered retro at the least, a big picture frame window right in the center of the living room. It overlooked a yard so big I only thought existed in lifestyles of the rich and famous. I didn't know it then but from the moment I met her that Lady (whom I would come to call Aunt Daisy) would change my life. Forever. As she and my parents sat and talked, I couldn't help but to wonder who she was, what she had done and why her name was on so many awards throughout the house. Even as a child of ten I knew she had to be very important, smart and stylish. Just like the women I had seen on television.

Even while sipping her tea she did it with such style and grace, I felt like I was in a movie. Coming from a chicken farm in Spearville, Louisiana, to see such a thing was rare.

Living Behind the Shadow

By the time we left her house, I knew I wanted to go to Aunt Daisy's house every day after school, so I made sure to get approval from both her and my parents. They said, "Yes." While at Aunt Daisy's we would have an afternoon snack, water the plants and she would give me private etiquette classes; then I would help her prepare dinner and set the table. My parents would sometimes join us. I would go to her house every day after school and on some Fridays, I would get to spend the night. The great times I had with her all week now spilled over into my Saturday morning because I woke up to a grand breakfast prepared by Aunt Daisy, was the norm. After we ate, she would hand me the newspaper and I would sit on the floor next to her wheelchair and read about the happenings in Little Rock. She would say slow down, pronounce your words just don't read them. Sometimes, when I didn't think she was listening I would catch her starring out of the big window in the living room. I often wondered what she was thinking and why sometimes she got so sad. Sometimes it seemed as thou she was miles away. I would call her name and she would look at me and smile.

Living Behind the Shadow

Sometimes she even talked about her childhood and how she longed to really know who her family was. Aunt Daisy didn't grow up around her biological family that is why she longed so much to know about her family. She was raised by neighbors because her mother had been beaten, raped and killed by two white men and nothing was done about it. The people told her father to leave town, so he left his daughter with the neighbors with plans to come back and get her, but did never had that opportunity, so she was raised by another family.

So, when my family moved to Little Rock and my dad, her brother made contact with her, she was so happy. When we arrived, the first question she asked my dad was, "How do you spell your last name?" He said, "G A T S O N," and her response was, "I found my family."

Even though I loved going to my Aunt Daisy's house after school, as I got old it seems that I sometimes think I took sitting at her feet for granted. If I knew then what I knew now, I would have taken a little bit more time, slowed down and read a few more lines.

Living Behind the Shadow

Class! Class! Mrs. Anware, my sixth-grade teacher exclaimed, "get yourselves together this assignment is very important." As she began to talk about the civil rights movement, I wondered why my aunt's name had not been mentioned. As she went on and on, I slowly raised my hand and said in my sixth grad voice, "Mrs. Anware, can I bring my Aunt?" "CIeandrea, who is your aunt?" "Daisy Bates," I proudly said with a huge smile on my face. She said, "You know Mrs. Bates?" I responded by saying, "YES! She is my aunt. My teacher said, "We would love to have her come to our class!" So began the story of my life and why I always received A's in History.

That next week my aunt was at the school and everyone was very excited, rushing around, making a big fuss. Besides my class it was several other teachers and classes that came to hear my aunt speak. It felt like the whole sixth grade class had been packed in my little classroom. While my aunt spoke, they seemed to hang on to every word. She left the students with these three points before she completed her speech: never to hate it took too much energy, listen to your parents and to always read. She said, "EDUCATION IS FREEDOM!" I went home that day feeling like a super star and like a celebrity. I told my aunt how I was feeling and she responded to me saying, "You are, we all are because celebrity status is nothing more than a mindset."

It went on like that for me pretty much my whole school life but nothing will ever top my senior year.

CHAPTER 4

Recognizing the Legacy

My senior year, 1996 was the year I found out who I was. I began to realize what my aunt had been telling me all this time about me. This year changed me. It changed the way I saw life and even though I tried my best to run from who I was and who God wanted and needed me to be. I soon found out that destiny will find you no matter what you want. God's will for your life will always win.

It was a day I would never forget. My teacher then was Mrs. Allen. I loved her, she really cared about her students. The assignment was an English paper, but somehow to bring my aunt was better than a report. This time instead of my class, the whole school would be participating because Daisy Bates the famous Civil rights leader from Little Rock, Arkansas was coming to the school to speak. The students learned that she was my aunt. I remember before the program started, I noticed a run in my stocking. I showed Mrs. Allen and she gave me an extra pair she kept in her desk. I felt like that little girl meeting her for the first time all over again. My hands were shaking, knees knocking, and sweating. I was a mess. As the bell rang, I went to my locker excited and nervous at the same time, people I didn't know was smiling and wishing me luck on what I thought was going to be a quick question and answer session. My teacher saw me at my locker and told me how pretty I was and I calmed a little but not much, and coming from her that meant a lot. I closed my locker walked down the hall and walked into the auditorium and it was empty! Maybe this wouldn't be as big as I thought. As soon as I begin to take long deep breaths and as I sat down, that's when I heard it.

Living Behind the Shadow

An announcement that Daisy Bates the Civil Rights Leader was in the building and if you want the chance to hear her speak to come to the main auditorium.

Not only was the auditorium packed, I also learned that I would be interviewing my aunt, asking her questions. By this time, Aunt Daisy had more than a few strokes and some found it difficult to understand her, so I would also be interpreting for the audience. It was my turn. My turn to make her proud and to make her smile. My job was to remember what I had been taught, remember to pronounce my words, sit up with my head high and to REMEMBER WHO I WAS.

As she began to smile, I calmly introduced myself and told why we were here.

My aunt began to speak about the movement and her busy life back and forth from Washington, the newspaper and some of her personal struggles during the way. She spoke about change and how you have to stand up no matter the cost. She shared about how important it is to be different and never blend in to be a part of the crowed. She talked about how she stood alone many days and

Living Behind the Shadow

how you have to be willing to forgive and move on. That day I received an A on my paper.

Believe it or not I was a freshman in college still sitting at her feet, still reading the paper at the foot of her wheelchair.

CHAPTER 5

How Did I Get Off Track?

After all that I have gone through, crazy marriages, unfulfilling relationships, black sheep and all I still came out on the winning side. I have learned many lessons, but one in particular is that in life man's opinion doesn't count. Not when it comes to your life. So called friends and family will have a field day with your life, but you have to stop giving them access.

Living Behind the Shadow

I remember the Pastor I was in relationship with, not married to, just dating. A lot of you think you're married and you're not. If you get the paper it means nothing. Marriage is a mindset and his mind wasn't set. Anyways, I remember we got back from church one Sunday and he had preached heaven down, he threw a box of half eaten chicken at me. He had hell in his heart. He was married on paper but not in his heart. Years earlier my Aunt Daisy had taught me about men like him, but somewhere along the line I forgot about me and when you forget about you, you leave room for the many demons to enter your life. I allowed situations and their issues to drag me down. I set up a permanent subscription to their problems without even thinking twice about how it would affect me.

You need to learn how to choose you. It's so easy for others to mentally rape you. They sit on your heart and pull at your dreams, hopes, expectations and desires and watch you give birth to despair and nurse hate. It drains you. Like most victims of physical rape, you hide but in the spirit. That's the worst kind because now you are ashamed.

Living Behind the Shadow

The noises of life are now so loud, you can no longer hear I AM MORE.

It's time to break out, lose and free. How did I do it? How did I overcome? Fasting, praying letting go of the poison some of us might call low self-esteem. I found me through all of the heartache, mess of ministry and even my aunt's death. I found

Daisy Bates loved hard. She pushed so she wouldn't be forgotten. Her works were many and at times her own fellow fighters would turn against her. A few sideline back deals were made concerning her home. This same home that I grew to love going to and spending time with my Aunt Daisy, at the age of 12 would no longer be the same for me.

It was now a house. A Shell of brick and memories. I remember while sitting at the foot of her wheelchair she told me to always remember not only who I was but who's I was. A strong black little girl who could grow up and create change. I believed her. Because of her teaching I have evolved into a new dimension of self-worth and power.

Living Behind the Shadow

It is imperative to know who you are. From a good wife to first lady I had it all figured out? I figured wrong. It's not about me, it never was. It was about growth the whole time.

Evolving into something bigger than me. For some of you, life is a stage play. You have a manager who keeps you in order. You do and say what is expected, you forget a line or move in the wrong spot someone is there to put you back in your place. It's all a lie. Your life is a lie. You are playing a part you were given and not living what you were called.

You have to break free from your script. There is something powerful in you. You have been called to a higher level in God. Did He not create you? He has an obligation to bring you into your greater, you are a new creation. Believe in you and walk in the new you.

I did as many do, I tried to depend on people, places and things to validate my position in life. I came to realize that I was too busy complaining to see the bigger calling and the plans God had for my life. Once I realized my self-worth that my Aunt Daisy had been sharing with me all those times I sat at her feet, I would have realized it sooner. We all have our path that life takes us through, but there are many times when we endure the things, we endure because of our inability to see. We are blinded to what's truly ahead for us because we are looking at our now and not into our future, nor looking at the things established that allows us to properly grow. Our eyes have to be opened as well as our spirits.

I spent so much time looking back over the situation with my husband, I remember so many questions I would ask myself. I was in a place where I continued looking back with the questions of why? I would ask things like, "What's good about this man? What happened? Why did I even marry him?" Many of these questions were pointed back to myself. I suffered from low self-esteem and began to question my own existence. This is a spirit that is heavy in the earth realm. Low self-esteem destroys people and the assignment God has placed over their lives. When you don't know who you are, this spirit is able to overtake you and distract you from your purpose in life. It causes you to form relationships that are not ordained by God. Relationships are just created, but they aren't Godly Connections or Kingdom Connections. I had to learn to stop looking back and grieving those things that I knew was destroying my spirit man and the divine purpose.

Change was necessary. I had to get out. I had to take authority over this spirit of low self-esteem and take the steps necessary to get me and my boys out of this situation. I could no longer endure the abuse. Stepping out was very uncomfortable and there were moments where I questioned if I was doing the right thing. You will go through days where you will question yourself even though deep inside you know you're doing the right thing? You will question if you really heard God or am, I operating in my own will and power? I distinctly remember I heard the Lord say to me, "Don't die at the exit door." He was speaking to me and not the people. That message couldn't be denied. The blood of my self-inflicted wound was spilling out and now I had to fix it.

CHAPTER 6

Where is the Help?

For me, church was not the answer. I wasn't ready. All our lives we are taught that if we attend church everything will be fixed. This is not true. Just going to church isn't going to fix you, you have to want to be fixed and your heart has to be turned toward God and your will has to be in alignment with God. You have to develop your own relationship with God and this can happen anywhere because God is everywhere. Congregating with genuine saints will help you, but you have to show up before your spiritual surgery will begin. You have to get to a place where you want it. You have to choose to transform or stay stagnate where you are.

God is patient and knows all things concerning us, and we will never waste His time. Humans are different. They aren't as patient, they don't know everything and often times, they may think they know what you are dealing with and give you advise that isn't relevant. The best thing to do is get in the presence of God and pour out your heart and give it all to Him. Then, sit and listen for His voice. Because people (humans) are impatient, they may be frustrated with you if you ask them to pray for you and you don't follow their instruction. They will begin to feel like you are wasting their time and may let you know they feel you are wasting their time. This may make you feel worse or even backslide, so the best person to take your cares to is God Himself.

Breaking free is a process and for some the process may take longer than others. Some may even say, don't ask people to pray for you if you don't plan to follow the plan of God. It sounds harsh but it's true, people really feel their time is wasted and feel that because they were delivered

Living Behind the Shadow

in a certain time period, they feel that others too should be delivered in a certain time. Once one's eyes have been opened, their focus intensify and fear will evaporate and the person will strive for change and not be afraid to seek it. They will begin to run after it and with the help of the Lord, they shall obtain it.

As your eyes open to reveal to you what you have been enduring, God will begin to move you to another level in Him. You have to be willing to move when God moves. Don't sit in the same position after He moves you. It's ok to move forward, even in fear. You can be afraid but only for one point two seconds. Don't sit in fear. If you sit there you get comfortable and it's easy to lay there. It's important to learn when to get up and get free.

We all have a destiny and a purpose. There is so much more at stake that the enemy desires to keep us from. The assignment you have been given is more than sitting in a building Sunday after Sunday.

You want the answer to the secret? Most times Pastors want you there for numbers. In fact, to some your offering isn't a big deal. The look of the church being full is what they want. So, they need you. If transformation happens it happens if not, it's not their issue. In their eyes a full church is a successful church. Your spirit is of non-importance.

Now don't get me wrong, every church or leader isn't like this. It's up to you to pray and seek God on where you should go and how to tell the difference. God is more than cars, clothes, houses, money. Now, He will provide you with these things but understanding your assignment comes first.

CHAPTER 7

Moving Past the Hurt and Brokenness

Did I mention I had paid all of the bills? He could have let me go during the beginning of the month when I had a little change. Oh well, I was broke and here I was with a U-Haul loaded with everything I had accumulated in almost four years of marriage and all the belongings of mine and my sons.

On moving day, my boys were at school and I was my myself loading this truck. My spirit was weak and I felt numb to the entire situation, I was truly broken from within. This is what I told him after my spirit felt like it had been pulled out of my body. I'm ready to leave this place of brokenness and get my feathers together and make wings.

Something happened when I looked at the last thing, I had to move my boy's beds. It was something that I didn't feel over the course of the last couple of days, it was anger. I was angry. I was angry looking at my boy's beds because my children had to suffer yet again because of me. My prescription to another man's issues had affected them and I was mad.

During my club hopping, weed smoking, drinking days I came across people who still showed love in spite of my problems and their problems. When I didn't have money for my favorite drink, they had me! Street love, is a love that will never be understood by many because they haven't been in that area.

I had friend cousins in the street who would make sure I was "straight" or "good" but now here I was, a "Pastor's Wife," homeless, broke,

Living Behind the Shadow

confused and broken. Now here I was with only twenty dollars in my pocket after I had sung heaven down, preached to thousands because of the television ministry, the niece of a Major Civil Rights leader, and in need. No one was around. I may have had the look but no understanding of the true meaning of who God truly was. This is the case for many. You smile as if everything is ok and as if you are truly happy, but that is not the case. You laugh with your church members, friends, and people at work but on the inside, you are a broken mess.

I came to realize and learn that God specializes in brokenness. He has to break you in order for you to be rebuilt. I had gotten so angry and frustrated about my situation. I was not only upset with myself for the choices I made, but I was even more angry at this person who I gave my all to. I was all in and I gave all; spiritually, physically and mentally. Not to mention financially. I received a substantial amount of money from a settlement and all except for a few hundred went to business ventures; funeral homes, car lots, church – but they never worked. All this money was wasted. God had removed His hand from this man and I saw there was nothing left. Not even the residue to prove He was once there.

I found myself in his living room in tears. My anger had almost gotten the best of me. I heard a voice that said burn this place to the ground. I started to pray. In my anger I told God I was done. I had been the best I knew to be and look what you gave me. A so-called man of God who my spirit has been in battle with since we were united by paper. I was treated better in the streets. I had one too many abusive relationships and I was done. Then the Holy Spirit reminded me that God had nothing to do with the man I choose. I never really prayed about him, I was so set on changing and coming out of the life of being in the club and trying to hang with cousins who were dealing drugs. I realized then, I had been running, I hadn't been delivered or free. I was hiding from myself.

I told God right then that I needed help. I told Him, "If you don't send me an angel right now, I'm done with you and your confused people. I am better off where I was." I then started listening to the lies of the Devil who was trying to convince me that my children, Samuel and Emanuel, didn't really need me. I began to believe that they would be better off without a mother because after all, I couldn't even keep a roof over their heads. I struggled with being able to tell the difference between real or counterfeit. I was emptying out all that was in my spirit and pouring it out to the Lord, letting Him know that I truly needed Him at this moment. I believe I was at rock bottom and completely broken, but do you know this is when the Lord is now able to work His miracles? When I finished telling God what I was going to do my eyes were so red and swollen from crying I could hardly see. We have to get out of ourselves and get to a point where we surrender. We have to get to a place where we can no longer move forward in our own strength and allow the Lord to move us forward through His strength and His strength only.

My miracle came as soon as I stood up and walked outside. He arranged it that a man whom He instructed to help a lady with a U-Haul to walk down the road at that exact time. God sent me the exact help I needed and sent me the angel I requested Him to send. From that day forward, I learned to trust the move. God was showing me that even in my anger, He was there and He had my back. He had a plan for my life and an assignment that needs to be fulfilled. Now I press toward the mark of completeness and work hard to complete the assignment God has entrusted me with. I know He is with me and it is heart's desire my to operate in obedience to His spirit.

CHAPTER 8

It's Not Over Yet

My story isn't over, it's just beginning. R.A.W. Ministries was established and the ministry is growing and I still preach God's Word. In 2017, R.A.W. Ministries grew from being a monthly program to a church congregation with members and it's old building to worship in. In order to promote the ministry, I struggled getting my announcements on the air because I couldn't afford the fees. God fixed that too. I am one of the morning Gospel hosts for a radio station in the Little Rock area. Now, I am responsible for sharing Gospel music, church announcements, local news, weather and events with faithful listeners two days a week. I love it.

God's process of healing and rebuilding is in full effect. He is working miracles out on my behalf and speaking loud and clear. My ears are tuned into His voice and I know He has a Word for His people. I seek spirituality now more than anything. I don't look to be validated by man because I am approved by God.

After leaving in that truck that day, I didn't know where to go, so I went where I knew I would always be welcomed, I went home to mom and dad. I lived with my parents for less than two months before I was able to get a small three-bedroom apartment, big enough for me and my two boys. My parents were a great help, they paid half of the rent until I could handle it on my own. I struggled and at one point and was on food stamps to make sure that the refrigerator stayed full. It seemed like every part of my life was affected, but I fought. My lights were turned off, my gas tank was on E. I understood that it was all a part of my process, so I pressed forward to get the healing I know I needed and pressed to

Living Behind the Shadow

rebuild according to the way God wanted me to. I was willing to give myself, my whole self to Christ. It wasn't until I came into this mindset and only then that change began to take place.

Throughout my life, I made many mistakes. So many I can't count. I choose not to speak on them either only because by speaking about them, it will affect others in a negative way. Just know I my mistakes were many. I kissed many frogs and hugged many snakes, but God had my name on His mind the entire time. I came out better. Many of the decisions I made affected my children and they suffered too, but I declare that healing for them shall come as well.

I often think and have been told by certain family members that if I had been "a better mother" they wouldn't have had the struggles they experienced. Samuel and Emanuel's dad was the most negative; at times he made me feel like the worst mother on earth, but again I had to remember that hurt people, hurt people. He had issues himself that he hadn't dealt with and because he didn't know how to handle his issues, the boys got mixed up in the anger he felt toward me.

Forgiveness was key. I had to forgive the family members who spoke these unkind words, I had to forgive the boy's father, but most of all I had to forgive me. I had to quickly remind myself that forgiveness of myself is the most important gift I can give myself. It happened, I could have done it better, I didn't, move on. My boys love me and know that I will always be there for them no matter what. Yes, we have had our ups and downs, but through it all, our relationship has grown stronger too. We can't allow the words of others to bring shame. We are healed and moving forward to rebuild.

The Lord has showed me that the best way to deal with things now is to go into my prayer closet and sincerely pray for them. That's how you are elevated in the spirit. I don't focus on the family that don't speak to me, the cousins who look at me like I am invisible, I just pray for them and keep on moving.

CHAPTER 9

Aunt Daisy's Lessons

Remember earlier, I said that I took the time I spent at Aunt Daisy's feet for granted. Well, it's now that I really realized how much I miss those times and realize how I should have cherished them more than I did. The childhood home my aunt taught me in was a comfort to me, but I no longer have access to it because of some things that occurred. Greed brings the worst out in situations and families. It's amazing how people will become opportunists and take advantage of you when you're at your lowest.

Living Behind the Shadow

My aunt's house was so uplifting. Always neat, yet inviting. Some of my best times were spent in the basement reading from the small library that was full of history. She had a small antique couch that I would lay on while sipping a glass of sweet tea she made fresh every day. I remember she had a lemon for the tea and a lemon for the cats. She told me if you brushed them with the lemon it made the cats coat shinny. I was never a cat person, but I did respect my aunt's cat; Pumpkin and Fluffy. The respect between myself and them went both ways, I respected them and they respected me, but we were never friends. One thing about it they knew my aunt loved them like her children, but never more than me.

I was taught so much by Aunt Daisy. I watched and I listened, most of all I learned. The work she did as a Civil Rights Leader was powerful and effective here in Little Rock. I saw her interact with many from her team. One thing I noticed is that many of those close to her ended up taking more than they were adding to. Many took advantage of her and I learned to keep my team small. Numbers do not matter, especially if they

Living Behind the Shadow

are corrupt and actually taking from the vision instead of adding to it. What matters is what they are bringing or adding to your life, vision and ministry.

Most times we will find we have a bunch of team members with no team. Don't allow the pettiness of people to push you out of the will of God. People can and will be fickle and sometimes even hateful. People will envy you based on skills, talents and abilities you possess or dislike you based on someone else's thoughts towards you. These are people to stay away from.

If you want to build, create and move when God speaks stay away from these people. They are spirit killers and are dangerous to your anointing and calling.

Aunt Daisy also taught me that no matter what you have, be ready to accept the move of God. You may not like it especially when you are going through difficult situations such as; death, divorce, sickness or any other storm you may be facing. These stressors are sometimes hard to overcome but it can be done. Personally, I had to accept the fact that I am not in charge, God is!

Living Behind the Shadow

We all have free will, but when God gives us an assignment, we now have a mandate to carry it out. We have to get rid of things that hinder us and walk in our assignment.

Being able to overcome an addiction is very important and these addictions often become the biggest obstacles or hinderance we face. You can be addicted to people, shopping, lying, gambling, food etc. Drugs are the first thing that most likely comes to mind when speaking of addictions. This is because that's mostly what has been taught. We have deceived ourselves because we don't read. Your Bible is literally a wealth of information but we feel like we need more. The Bible gives us all that we need, but people are always looking for more. What is more? Spirit guides. Horoscope. Psychics. Mediums. Life coaches (If not Biblically Based). None of these can replace what God can provide to us in His Word or through a personal relationship with Him.

These other things can be dangerous to your spiritual growth and commitment to Christ. Why? It's simple, they are deceptive conductor into an unknown spirit world. Yes, it exists. It existed in the days when Jesus walked the earth and it exist now. Be careful because although they make your flesh feel good, they will cause you to cry in the end. Most see that you are weak and vulnerable and you become a way of making money. Your soul is of no importance to people to use these alternative methods.

Do you want to know the plan of the enemy? We are told in the Bible that your enemy the devil is like a roaring lion seeking whom he may devour. That is his plan, to devour you. If he can distract you and pull you away from your assignment and your true calling, then he believes he has succeeded. This is what happened with me. I wasn't praying, I felt like I didn't belong anywhere. I was the laughing stalk of my family, most of them only spoke about me and not to me. They didn't help and actually just added to the duress in my life. I had to push through no matter what. It took a Jeremiah anointing to push through, but I pushed and I pushed and eventually, I made it. I know it can be done because I did it.

Living Behind the Shadow

I had to pursue, relate and release the things they hindered me. This is the recipe I used to heal and eventually walk into my purpose. First, you have to pursue the mind of God. Seek Him and determine what it is He has for you in your life. Seek your purpose and why He created you. Secondly, you have to relate to your past. You don't have to forget your past, but you do have to forgive and stop getting stuck because of your past. You can use your past as a gauge to see how far you have come, but you have to move forward into the new things of the Lord for your life. Life will be filled with both ups and downs. Learn at every level and keep moving. Finally, you have to be released from your former way of thinking. During this time of release, people will be removed from your life, this may also include some family. You have to seek the Lord on who you should remove from your life because some may be there to help and because of your past, you may not see that they are actually there to help you; but then these are those that may be on scene that are just there to see you in your pain and weakness to say, "I told you so." Allow God to truly lead you and bring understanding to why

Living Behind the Shadow

each person of your life is there. Some give you what you need all of your life, some give you enough to sustain you until God puts others in their place. Still be respectful but know when manipulation has stepped into the room, leave like the lady or gentleman that you are.

To family and those that know you may think you're messed up and look disfigured, but you have been delivered and in the Master's hands. God has taken His time and worked with your desire. That's all He needs. He has reshaped you, added and taken away. You just don't look the same. Don't worry, that's how God works. He heals you to the point where you don't even look the same. If family can't accept that then that's between them and God. Move on, your assignment is at hand. He has changed your outer and inner appearance; He has regulated your mind and now your heart is focused to hear His heart. Your ears are opened to hear His voice. You understand that He will sometimes change your direction to make you destination clear.

I got tired; I fell. My fall was great but I got up. I remembered His Word and knew that my steps

Living Behind the Shadow

are ordered by the Lord and because I am His greatest creation, He has an obligation to fulfill His will for my life. He is with us in every season of our lives, in the good time, in the up time, in the bad times and even in the down times. No matter what, He is there and He loves us as well in every state and season we are in too. Although you will encounter many seasons in life remember every season is about you and your elevation in God. If you are not together the assignment doesn't go through.

CHAPTER 10

She Led Me to Him

My aunt, Daisy Bates was my guide before I really understood who God, Christ Jesus was. I went to church; my parents were active in the church but I never understood fully why until she explained the motion and meaning of a relationship with God. No, she wasn't in church every Sunday, but her relationship with God was present and well seen. As I have said before, with the things she endured since childhood, a relationship with Christ was inevitable. She would tell me in life you give up or keep pushing. I chose to keep pushing. There are days when

Living Behind the Shadow

pain tries to take over me and take me out. Somedays life seems unbearable because it's not moving as fast as I want it to or think it should be moving. I just keep pushing. I remember who I am. I can't say it enough; you need to remember who you are and who's you are. You are God's creation and if you have become saved and living a life that is surrendered to Him, you are His child. You have an inheritance in God through Jesus Christ.

For so long my aunt lived in the shadow of her assignment. It was who she was, loneliness can and will be an issue. There will be days when you will feel like you aren't moving forward. Remember, you are what you have been called to do. You won't have many friends, deal with it. You are your assignment.

You will never live in the house of perseverance if the house was built in fear. Keep pushing. In order to build, you better know your purpose. It's necessary.

Learn to praise. Aunt Daisy, taught me to Praise God even in the rain. The rain brings a cleansing of your soul. Prepare your soil, your newness is

Living Behind the Shadow

trying to grow! You can only cover your pain for so long.

The last one rings home for me because at the age of 16, I tried to kill the body and soul God had blessed me with. I was unhappy, I felt alone. All of my friends seemed so happy. They were doing things on the weekend while my activities centered on church activities with teenagers who didn't even like me. I was often called stuck up. I just didn't fit in with them. I would remember being so happy "down home" with my grandparents and going to school with cousins, because I knew they understood me. All this was taken away when we moved to Little Rock.

When I was about six or seven, I had a feeling that something was about to change and I didn't like it. I will never forget the feelings I felt. My feeling proved right and we soon moved away. I missed my grandparents and my cousins. The first elementary school I attended was exciting only because of one of my teachers, Mrs. Brannon. I loved her; she made the days go by in a happy way. I remember we had to do a report and poster on saying no to drugs, my Uncle

Marcetti who lived with us, helped me. It was so good I and I received an award. That was a happy time.

My teacher was very proud of me. I came home and showed Uncle Marcetti my ribbon and he told me to remember this day and that one day I would need to say no to drugs. Somewhere along the line that day became mixed up in the haze of life. Weed, Ecstasy, Alcohol became cool with me. I lived a life of dating drug dealers, pastors and people you wouldn't believe. I lived.

My life is a testimony, truth be told, so is yours. We all have a past and a path the has led us to the place we are right now. Don't allow the spirit of intimidation to stop you from breaking out. Family will be your number one distraction. I can't tell you how many people who have told me they knew what they were supposed to do and that they knew their calling, but they were afraid because of people.

Let's look at this analogy of how spirits partner to wreak havoc in your life and cause a spiritual invasion. I was home and received a call from opportunity, but before I could pray about it, I saw impatience crepe through the window. Not only did impatience come but it was holding the hand of disappointment. My home was getting crowded so I opened the door and there was depression. I got weak so I stepped back in the house, laid down and realized hopelessness was lying beside me. I tried to get up to move, but fear was holding me down.

When I saw fear, I knew I had to get away. I closed my eyes and begin to pray and that's when I felt hope overtake them all. Then peace came in and brought joy, longsuffering and faith. With faith on scene, then I knew strength and patience wasn't far. They all made a circle around me and I knew protection had taken over.

I live because I trust the instruction of the highest God. I trusted because I saw the move of God on my aunt's life. I remembered her words and during the times I stayed away, many, many times but because He was in me, He had me and wouldn't let me go. Jesus Christ knows my name and I am grateful.

She was my greatest gift although I had to share her with the nation.

Living Behind the Shadow

So, it begins, my greatest accomplishment, my continuing, my life, my legacy begins. Living life with a full set of wings that at times seem too heavy but not impossible to fly. My children and parents the different phases of their lives keep me alert. They are my greatest reward, and I cherish being their mother. They are not without flaw, but I keep them lifted in prayer. No one can pray for them like I can. Samuel Cleodis and Emanuel Elijah, my gifts.

Mothers, giving up is not an option whether through adoption or birth. I am your example that prayer works.

CHAPTER 11

Block Out Noises of Negativity

I remember one day someone told me life wasn't about me, oh but it is. It's my life, on this earth I will not get another, so I chose to live it on my God given terms. Those you choose can be apart or they can use the exit door.

I am happy to show those who don't believe the door. We all have dealt with them one way or the other, those that are always seeing the negative and never the good. Those are signs that it's time to downsize.

When I finally got a building for my ministry, I dealt with a few of naysayers. Always negative, never positive. I had some come that started to help, but did not finish what they said they'd do, so I learned that I too had to ask for discernment and seek the Lord to see who was actually there because of Him and the Word being preached. Some will come for a season, help, learn and move on. Be grateful for what they contributed and even if it wasn't a great experience, be grateful for the lesson learned. Some come and go quick because they are searching for something and will never find it. Some will come and leave because of the Word being preached and their skeletons are being exposed and they aren't liking it, so they leave. They will use excuses like, "I need more or my season is up," to leave when in fact they are afraid of the work that is required for elevation. Don't get upset. Those people are nothing more than church hoppers. Unless they allow God to transform their heart, they will continue to search and go from place to place always looking for something. It really hurts when these individuals are family, but keep pushing, it does get better. God will send what and who you need to sustain you.

I remember a snake I once dated. He had been drinking and later I learn he also snorted cocaine. He came to my place I had in Eldorado, Arkansas. He was full of what I call incomplete Demons. I'll tell you more about those in my next book. Anyways, he was trying to get in the apartment screaming beating the door down, cursing and just acting like Satan himself. I was afraid to open the door, but more afraid not to. As soon as I did, I knew I was in trouble. The look he gave me was indescribable. His eyes were black and behind them nothing, he had scars and scratches all over his face that I hadn't seen before. He was very drunk and upset and his veins were popping out of the hands that were now tearing at my clothes. I hollered no but it meant nothing to the human like figure in front of me. I had been praying that day and knew I needed a change in my life. I remembered reading that every knee had to bow to Jesus, so I begin to call on the name of Jesus. Knowing that even Demons had to become subject to Him.

As he tore at my clothes my shorts were almost down, I saw myself lying dead in that apartment and I remember thinking I'm not going out like this. He was high and way trying to rape me because he was erect. I said JESUS once. His nails are now scratching my skin and his hands are making their way to my neck, so I called out the name of JESUS a second time. Now, I'm fighting for my life. I'm was on the floor being drug through my apartment and I feared this would be the last place I would breathe. I cried out, "Jesus, Help Me!" Immediately, he went limp and began saying, "This is voodoo." He stopped pursuing me and left the apartment. I got up the lock the door and began to praise Jesus and thank Him for sparing my life.

Everyone has a map to freedom. Everyone's map is not the same, but the journey is always directed to the same place, to our Lord and Savior, Jesus Christ.

Living Behind the Shadow

Who hasn't been hurt in the church? In the street? When you receive your healing keep pushing, release yourself from it and move forward. You will find even those who are there with you will only go so far, but don't worry that's called conditional help. He will send those who are willing to go with you all the way. You won't be liked by all. Most of my mother's side don't speak to me. Flesh will hurt, but your spirit knows there is something more. Never be afraid of what other people think. In your walk of life, man's opinion does not count. Your newness won't allow anything less. Live free. You can't move forward wondering if you're meeting the standards of man.

Be aware of those who have been sent to break you. My earliest memory is of a snake talking to me when I was about four or five. It was a Viper, he told me that if I allowed him to, he would use me greatly in his kingdom, but right now he wasn't able to touch me. I remember this! The enemy knows that one day you will lose sight of who you really are (Gods property) and use this to his advantage. Take control of what may have been spoken to your bloodline. Some entities feel as though they are still connected because you haven't told them any different. Sometime you have to dismantle what family have built in the spirit. That can only be done through spiritual authority. Use it.

Know who you are. It can't be said enough.

Aunt Daisy was my teacher and the world was my classroom, sometimes my work was and still is difficult and uncomfortable, it is necessary. It is necessary for the upkeep of a nation our children call home. If you handle your assignment correctly, you can change the world. No matter your age, race, social status or level of education you are a part of a classroom where you never stop learning.

I have touched fear; I know it exist but I do not become its friend and I pushed past it because I know it was tempting to hide because it's something I cannot see. My aunt would be proud, but not content. She would tell me I haven't done enough, no excuses. If I could I would ask how? How do I make such an impact the way she did? How do I become better? How do you get a nation

Living Behind the Shadow

out of their own shadow and under the voice of God?

Keep pushing until you break through and free. Remember you are more than what they think. At times I feel as though I stood in her shadow and didn't understand why I went through the things I did. I had to realize I choose my destiny, bad decisions, brokenness, abuse and all. I stood in her shadow but her words made me close. The words she spoke to me, now comfort me and encourage me to do better and press to make a difference in this world.

CHAPTER 12

Moving Beyond the Shadow

In 2015, I did a DVD titled, Focusing on the Wrong Thing. It is so important that we keep our focus in alignment with God's focus. His will and focus is the only one that should matter. By staying focused on Him and seeking direction, your assignment has to come forth. My aunt's assignment was to change the nation through one move. That move was never to take no for an answer. She knew change had to take place and she knew that it was up to her to change it and because of that one act, she changed the world, literally.

Living Behind the Shadow

Ask yourself, what is my assignment and what am I focused on right now? If not now, then when? If not me, then who? I know it's a cliché but it's what we must live by. In order for this to work we must have faith. It is important to keep our faith in a place that we can always go back to and build upon it. Never keep your faith confined. When faith is confined, it is limited, small, tight, and compact you will never be comfortable enough to go higher. If I have a supernatural faith, this is when there is enough space to move and walk in confidence and authority.

I will never surrender to what I go through because I understand that things have to happen in order for me to exercise my faith and grow. Maturity comes through the trials we face. Paul was locked up and in prison, but several of the letters he wrote were written while in prison, which proved that the physical man can be locked up, but his spirit was free. My condition is what causes me to pray and my condition frees me because I know the power of God. I understand that what I'm going through will only give me strength. When I understand this my spirit is feed and not my flesh. When my spirit is feed, I will not be broken or spiritually malnourished.

I have realized that in my past, I choose to leave before my assignment was completed. I never carry it out and so I never understood the move of God for my life. I wasn't clear about my assignment and I lived in a 'what if' state of mind.

It all comes down to faith. Faith exemplifies love, and without love there can be no power. Without power, I cannot have faith. It takes power to believe something that you cannot see, so faith is the key to living out my assignment and staying out of the shadows.

It's important to understand that in order to exceed my level of faith; I must move past what I think, how I feel or even what I am familiar with and choose to walk by faith and not by sight. It is not about knowledge, but about wisdom. Move past how do you feel and move past what you see and press forward to finish your assignment. If I want to live a complete life in God, I have to learn how-to live-in faith.

Again, Paul was locked up and in a dark place. He was confined and uncomfortable but it bought greatness out of him. Fight for your deliverance. At some point of finishing out your assignment you will learn to wait. Galatians 6:9 tells us, to be not weary in well doing, for in due season you shall reap if you faint not. Due season mean when God gets ready. Due season doesn't always mean a yes. Sometimes a no from God is a divine intervention to redirect us from we think we want to what He wants for us. When you're free everything about you will change.

My Aunt would tell me to continue to live free... out of the shadows. Outside of the thoughts and opinions of others and a life submitted and surrendered to the will of God Himself.

POEM

I was at home and I had received a call from opportunity, but before I could pray about it, I saw impatience creep through the window.

Not only did impatience come in but it was holding the hand of disappointment.

My home was getting crowded, so I open the door and there stood depression.

I got weak and didn't feel like going out of the house, so I went back in and laid down only to realize hopelessness was lying next to me.

Living Behind the Shadow

I wanted helplessness to move but fear was holding him down.

I had to get away, so I closed my eyes and begin to pray.

While I was praying, I saw hope overtake them all.

Peace walked in and brought joy.

I saw long-suffering walking in with faith and with faith came strength, while holding the hand of patience.

They all made a circle around me and when I saw protection, I knew I was safe.

They took my hand and I turned around and saw grace and mercy, I felt so much better.

I said, "Lord how can I repay you for the gifts you have brought me?"

He said share them with others.... He said, "One more gift I need to give you, boldness."

Living Behind the Shadow

I knew that fear kept looking for me, but love spoke up and told me, "Wait because the souls of many were in trouble."

Boldness told me, "You will probably have to deal with dislike." But humbleness held my hand and handed me peace and favor.

Love looked me in the face and said, "I will cover it all."

R.A.W.
REAL
ANOINTED
WORTHY

IF IT AINT RAW IT AINT REAL

www.ingramcontent.com/pod-product-compliance
Lightning Source LLC
LaVergne TN
LVHW051511070426
835507LV00022B/3043